Matt & Ben
Damon & Affleck

ON AND OFF SCREEN

An Unauthorized Biography by
Sheryl Altman

HA!
Harper
Active™

ACKNOWLEDGMENTS

Thanks to everyone who's supported me in my writing career: my HarperCollins crew; Marion Landew for teaching me to live out loud on paper; my family, The Kahns and The Berks, for always being my cheering section; Buddy, Richie, and Ceil Stein, and the rest of the Riverdale Press crew for giving me my first byline at age 17; and last, but never least, my husband, Peter (who's hunkier than Matt and Ben combined!).

—Sheryl

HarperCollins®, ☕®, and HarperActive™ are trademarks of HarperCollins Publishers Inc.

Matt Damon & Ben Affleck: On and Off Screen
Copyright © 1998 by HarperCollins Publishers Inc.

Printed in the United States of America. For information address HarperCollins Children's Books, a division of HarperCollins Publishers, 10 East 53rd Street, New York, NY 10022.

ISBN: 0-06-107145-5
2   3   4   5   6   7   8   9   10
❖
First Edition, 1998

Visit us on the World Wide Web!
http://www.harperchildrens.com

Matt & Ben
Damon & Affleck

*To Holly, my partner in crime
and writing sublime*

Dear Friends:

I have always believed that two heads are better than one.

Case in point: my tenth-grade bio class. Mrs. Reid asked me to dissect a frog. The ickiness factor was enough to send me cowering behind the Bunsen burners in the back of the room. But The Teach stood tough: "Cut Kermit!" was the order. My friend Rob came to the rescue. He sliced and diced with the expertise of George Clooney on ER—and we've been buddies ever since.

Over the years, my pals have always been my supporting cast. How many nights did Noreen, my buddy since ninth-grade homeroom, answer the phone at 2 AM to give me a refresher course in The Rules? How many times did my career compadre Stacy and I commiserate over cold pizza and Diet Coke? How many midnight runs for final exam fuel did I make to Denny's with Pam, my college roommate and buddy since babyhood?

Sometimes it takes a friend to make you see not just the way things are, but the way they could be. Matt Damon has this in Ben Affleck. He went to Ben with a wacky idea for a movie, and Ben—instead of writing him off like everyone else had done—helped Matt write it.

Holly, my Affleck-esque amiga, does this for me. We make a great pair. I hope someday we'll write our own Oscar-worthy screenplay. Who knows, maybe Claire Danes or Winona Ryder will play the lead. And when that happens, we'll thank Ben and Matt for the inspiration. It's one thing to act like a friend and another to be the real thing. They are the real thing.

—SHERYL

CONTENTS

CHAPTER 1

America's Most Wanted

"Ben and Matt? Hey, aren't they those ice cream guys from Vermont?"
—Ben

You'd have to be living on Mars to NOT know the names of Hollywood's two newest hotshots—Matt Damon and Ben Affleck. Although they are way too modest to admit it, even they are aware that they're (as Jim Carrey might say) "smokin'!"

The pair is everywhere: on magazine covers (*Entertainment Weekly*, *Vanity Fair*, *People*); on talk shows (an entire hour on *Oprah!*); and even in the casts of this summer's anticipated blockbuster movies (Ben in *Armageddon* and Matt in *Saving Private Ryan*).

Why all the buzz about these boy wonders?

Well, for starters, they're drop-dead gorgeous: Ben's rippling muscles and Matt's sexy smirk can reduce any girl to a quivering mound of Jell-O. But looks aren't everything: add Ivy League smarts, natural-born talent, and razor-sharp repartee to the mix and you've got one—better make that two!—irresistible packages.

Sure, critics tried to write them off as the dreamboats du jour at first—they could have easily fit into the Hollywood Frat Pack. But these *Good Will* wunderkinder are different. At twenty-something, they are extremely resourceful, possess an integrity way beyond their years, and have a well-honed instinct for navigating the shark-infested waters of the movie biz. Quite simply, Ben and Matt refuse to sell out.

"I'm certainly never going to be anyone's sex symbol," Matt humbly told *Vanity Fair.* "It's easy to get caught up, but you have to be yourself," Ben chimed in. And they mean it. They could have handed over their screenplay to any number of studios, but instead they held out for one that would be true to their vision. While other leading men stock their closets with Calvin and Armani once they make it big, Ben and Matt have opted to keep their low-profile baggy jeans, clunky work boots, and seven-day stubble ("I never shave unless I have to!" explains Ben). And supping at Spago? Fah-ged-aboud-it! These show-biz bigwigs prefer to belly up to the all-you-can-eat surf-and-turf bar at their local Sizzler's.

Maybe that's their greatest appeal— they're REAL. Despite the fame, fortune, fans, and now their new pal Oscar, they've remained the same nice guys they've always been. Above all, they're still best buds and have been since their childhood days in Cambridge, Massachusetts. Just yesterday, they were a couple of kids dreaming of the big time, "taking business lunches" in the high school cafeteria, and rehearsing their goofy Academy Awards acceptance speeches (mouthwash bottle in hand) in front of the bathroom mirror. They both struggled with acting careers and college, and survived the "lean, mean Spam cuisine years," according to Ben.

It's been such a whirlwind year for them both. Perhaps somebody should pinch them (any volunteers?). "I can't believe it," Matt says of how far they've come. But he and Ben always believed in themselves and their abilities. "Our moms used to say, 'Why don't you two just become doctors?'" he recently told *Interview*. "I'm glad we didn't listen." Us, too.

CHAPTER 2

Kids in Cambridge

How did these Cambridge cuties first meet?

Matt: *"I was pretty much forced into hanging out with Ben."*

Ben: *"Oh yeah. And Matt was a breakdancer at the time."*

No matter how much these two vary the story of how they first met, one detail remains consistent: their moms can take credit. Ben and Matt grew up two blocks apart on Pearl Street in middle-class Cambridgeport, where their moms—a professor of early childhood education and an elementary school teacher—became fast friends, forcing the boys to play together.

When they first met, Ben was only eight and Matt was ten, but they shared a love of Little League which helped bridge the age difference. Matt claims to have been the best pitcher in town. Although if you ask Ben, "He never struck me out once. The achievement in Little League grows exponentially with each passing year," he jokes.

Even then, Matt liked Ben's playful prankster side, while Ben liked having an older friend to fend off bullies. "Ben used to ring my doorbell and then cower on the other side of the street, because he was afraid of the little kids at this school right next door," Matt recalls. Matt understood this behavior. His own big brother had always been there to look out for him. "[My brother] kept me in line my entire life. It was nice to have someone who looked up to ME for a change."

Double Trouble

For as long as both friends can remember, they called each other the "warrior" and the "clown." Matt was the oh-so-serious man with a plan; Ben was the practical joker. "Even back then, he was a charming bastard," Matt says of his best bud. "I remember exactly what he was like: gregarious, outgoing. It's no surprise that he grew up to be the totally obnoxious guy he is now."

Their childhood, they both admit, was "pretty normal." Matt's mom, who had once written a book on war play and violence in cartoons, encouraged him to use his brains instead of his brawn. No G.I. Joes or action figures for this kid! "Growing up for me was like you'd get some blocks and then you'd have to go make up a game. I was always making up stories and acting out plays; that's just the way I was raised."

Though his mom and dad divorced when he was just a toddler, Matt's dad "had a *Leave It to Beaver* attitude of how life should be. . . . It just didn't work out." Matt remembers once telling his dad what he wanted to be when he grew up: "I was originally going to be a basketball player.

Tiny Archibald was my favorite player—he's called Tiny because he's only six foot one." Upon hearing this, the senior Damon sat his son down for a heart-to-heart. "He said, 'I'm the tallest Damon ever to evolve and I'm five eleven,'" Matt recalls. "He told me there was no way I'd ever play in the NBA. I gave up basketball at that moment and took up acting."

Ben's choice to act at a young age was also strongly influenced by his father: "My dad was in a theater company in Boston for a long time, so I was always around that stuff. I guess it rubbed off." But Ben always liked the idea of becoming a film star more than he liked the idea of becoming a big Broadway star. "When I was growing up, I thought *Back to the Future* was the best movie ever," he told *GQ*. "I am not a kid who was weaned on Fellini."

Neither of the boys' moms was thrilled by her son's decision to be in films, but the guys stood their ground. "Matt and I were very straightforward about it," Ben insists. "In fact, I remember trying to convince Matt's mom that not everybody in Hollywood was a total liar and scum."

When did the worried parents realize

that the dynamic duo wasn't (as Ben put it) "totally wacko"? When did they know for sure that the boys would stop at nothing short of seeing their dreams come true?

"When they saw that this wasn't some rebellious thing or childhood fantasy," Matt says. When they saw "we meant business."

Pop Quiz: *Sound Bites*

You imagine that you know these guys so well you could finish their sentences. So tell us, which one of the Wonder Boys had this to say?

1. "Success is not something I've wrapped my brain around."

2. "Forget money. We would have taken anything for this script. Like a piece of chicken."

3. "I feel like I've stepped into someone else's life. Who is that guy?"

4. "Not long ago, we couldn't get arrested in Hollywood."

5. "I think we just got everyone pretty well fooled and they made our movie."

6. "Sometimes I pull my hair out in front of the computer, watching the cursor

blink, and I can't think of a thing to write."

7. "People certainly weren't like, 'Okay, let's get these two knuckleheads to headline our movie.'"

8. "I appeal to record-store clerks with nose rings and tattoos."

9. "I'm begging to do *Fletch 3*!"

10. "The trouble with being an actor is it's difficult to feel like you own your own life."

Answers: 1. Matt; 2. Ben; 3. Ben; 4. Matt; 5. Ben; 6. Matt; 7. Matt; 8. Ben; 9. Ben; 10. Matt

CHAPTER 3

School Ties

So what were these guys really like in high school?

"We weren't the Wonder Twins or anything. Far from it." —Ben

Anyone who knew Matt and Ben back in those days would hardly have expected them to evolve into big-screen stud muffins. "We were so nerdy," Ben confessed to *Interview* magazine. "It's too embarrassing—let's change the topic."

Affleck and Damon, dweebs? Well, let's just say they weren't winning any popularity contests. Each day at Cambridge Rindge and Latin School, they'd hang together in the cafeteria holding "business lunches" and formulating their future plans to conquer Hollywood and the rest of the world, too. Classmates cracked up—these guys had some serious delusions of grandeur!

"We'd sit there with our trays and these crappy little 50-cent sandwiches and we'd say things like, 'We're going to be big actors! We're going to take the town by storm!'" Ben told the *Boston Phoenix*.

"'We're going to be huge!'" Matt chimed in. "Then we'd say, 'Okay, so how was Spanish today?'"

What they lacked in charisma (that came later!) they made up for in enthusiasm. Matt's first stage appearance was playing a samurai in a Kabuki play, recalls his high school drama teacher Gerry Speca. "He was this little dervish," Speca told *US* magazine. "Running around, rehearsing his part, all his moves, making sure everything was just right. Mary Kay Place [his *Rainmaker* costar] has talked about how generous and how hard he works, and all those qualities were in evidence when he was a kid."

So these two hotties didn't attend *your* high school. But how does your alma mater stack up to theirs in other ways?

· The Cambridge Rindge and Latin School is a "comprehensive urban high school" located in Cambridge, Massachusetts, just outside Harvard Square.

· About two thousand students, representing different races, ethnic groups, and languages, attend.

· The World Language Department teaches classes in Chinese, French, German, Italian, Portuguese, Russian, Spanish, and (what else?) Latin.

· Wanna tour Matt and Ben's old turf? Check out its official web site at *http://www.ci.cambridge.ma.us/~CRLS/Latin1/Crls.htm.*

On to Hallowed Halls

With their careers in a dry spell, both boys headed to advanced academia. According to Matt, "There isn't a college Ben hasn't gone to." So what if Ben liked "women and partying" more than cramming for exams? Can you blame him? "He's still the smartest guy I know—smarter than me and extremely well read," Matt insists.

Matt, however, knew exactly where he wanted to study: on the ivy-walled campus of Harvard.

"I loved Harvard," Matt says. "It was a huge part of my life." He left a few semesters short of graduation, when his career began to take off. "I still have time left and I want to go back when I get a chance," he says. "I keep in touch with all my college friends. I left because at nineteen I started working. What was happening was that I would keep coming back and I would almost get done with a semester and then I would be yanked out. But I thought career-wise, it was serving me well."

While there, he dabbled in drama: "I was totally into the Harvard theater scene. The last play I did was *Burn This*. I did it in Winthrop House. I did a Shepard play directed by David Wheeler. I did a play over at the North Theatre Company. But I really would have done more—I knew people who were doing like two and three shows a semester. College theater is fun—doing student-directed stuff is great because everyone gets in there together."

And of course, what he owes most to his higher ed is the germ of an idea for an Oscar-winning screenplay. Had it not been for Harvard and a tough creative writing class, *Good Will Hunting* would never have been written. "Some things in life are kismet," Matt says. "You spend your whole life going toward a goal, not knowing how to get there, and suddenly it all clicks."

Way-Cool Web Sites

http://www.harvard.edu/

http://hcs.harvard.edu/~demon/ The school's famous humor mag, *The Demon* (no, not *THE DAMON*!).

http://www.hcs.harvard.edu/~pudding/ Official site for the Hasty Pudding Theatricals, America's oldest theater company, made up of Harvard and Radcliffe students. They honor a female and male star every year— complete with a parade and lots of silly outfits. Past honorees have included the likes of Susan Sarandon, Tom Hanks, Whoopi Goldberg, Robin Williams, Cher, and Mikhail Baryshnikov. Could Matt and Ben be on the list soon?

CHAPTER 4

Good Role Hunting: Matt Makes It

"I worried about paying the rent sometimes. After five years of getting pummeled like George Foreman in the ring with Muhammad Ali, this is great." —Matt

Oprah called him "Hollywood's golden boy." *Vanity Fair* says he's tomorrow's Tom Cruise. People can't stop heaping praise on the hunky twenty-eight-year-old—and no one could be more deserving.

Despite his youth, he's paid his dues, polishing his craft in bit parts and learning the industry from the inside out at a very young age.

"I always knew I wanted to be an actor," Matt confides. "I told my mom, 'Someday I want to walk down the street and have people say, "There goes Matt Damon, the best there ever was."' And she said, 'Did I raise you? That's just an egomaniacal pipe dream.'"

But Matt held tight to these dreams. "When I was eight or nine, I was getting into children's theater groups, taking pantomime classes, and things like that," he says. "I got an agent when I was sixteen—I told my mom and dad, 'I'm ready to go pro.' As if I was a baseball player or something!"

Even back then, he idolized his buddy Ben, who was already in the biz. Ben had an agent because he'd done a PBS series in Boston. "He told me, 'No sweat, dude. I can get you an audition with my agent in New York,'" Matt recalls. So with the $200 he'd earned making a T.J. Maxx commercial, he bought a round-trip ticket to NYC. "The agent signed me, but it really took years for my career to kick in. So I went to college and waited for something to happen."

It did, in 1988. Matt was cast opposite Julia Roberts in his big-screen debut (not bad for his first time out!). But 1988's *Mystic Pizza* didn't exactly put Matt on the map. "I had one line," he recalls. "If you blinked, you missed it."

Another career catastrophe? "I have this horrible, embarrassing story," Matt confesses. "I told everyone I was going to New York to meet the president of Walt Disney—we were having a 'meeting.' I get there and it turns out I'm *not* meeting the president. It's an audition for *The Mickey Mouse Club*. Even more humiliating? They didn't even pick me to wear the ears!"

Although he'd already been in *Glory Daze*, *School Ties* (both with Ben), and *Geronimo*, the role that made Hollywood sit up and take notice was the Gulf War vet-turned-heroin addict in 1996's *Courage Under Fire*. He lost 45 pounds (starving himself down to 139 pounds) to look the part, and nearly killed himself in the process: "I got really sick," Matt told *Mr. Showbiz*. "I couldn't afford a nutritionist and my adrenal system—I overtaxed it. I was losing weight and running 12.8 miles a day. I ate nothing but egg whites and chicken, maybe one baked potato a day. I was under two percent body fat. I'd be sleeping and get flashes of heat and charges of adrenaline. My body thought the bear was chasing it."

But it was this role that ultimately caught the eye of director Steven Spielberg: he thought Matt would be great in his new movie, *Saving Private Ryan*. Just one prob: he worried the actor was too skinny!

"He met me over lunch with Robin Williams," Matt recalls. "Trust me—I can eat! He probably took one look at me and my girth and said, 'I'm sold!'"

And so are audiences who can't wait for Matt's next movie project. He has several in the works, and the offers keep pouring in. "When you've got a lot of chips, it's easier to keep winning," he told *Time*. "I don't want to be a flash in the pan. I don't want to lose it all. I don't want to let people down."

Fat chance. Maybe he should stop stressing and just listen to the advice of his actor pal Matthew McConaughey: "He told me, 'Just enjoy the ride.'" 'Nuf said.

Damon Data

Name: Matthew Paige Damon

DOB: October 8, 1970

Height: 5' 10"

Home turf: Cambridge, MA. After his parents split when he was just a tyke, he was raised in an experimental co-op where five families lived together under one roof.

Family ties: His parents are divorced. His dad was a stockbroker but is retired now. Matt lived with his mom, who was a professor of early childhood education.

Are there any more like him at home? Yes, he has a brother, Kyle, who's three years older and works as a sculptor.

All this and brains, too: Matt and Ben both went (along with Ben's brother, Casey) to Cambridge Rindge and Latin School. Matt then went on to Harvard University in Cambridge where he majored in English. He was just a few semesters away from receiving his bachelor's degree when he decided to leave.

His idols: Morgan Freeman ("the best actor in the country"), Robert Duvall ("he can make things happen without doing much"), Marlon Brando ("he had a discipline that was unmatched, but now he gets away with everything"), Robert De Niro, Dustin Hoffman, Denzel Washington, Mickey Rourke, Jon Voight, Robin Williams, Al Pacino. "I also think David Wheeler is the best acting teacher in the country. Pacino goes to him. He teaches a class at Harvard called Intro to Acting for undergrads—he got his hands on me when I was seventeen. He's just extraordinary."

His appeal: "Matt's got the gift—and he's a writer in his own right. That makes him special." —Francis Ford Coppola, director of *The Rainmaker*

"There's something so apple pie about him. You know he was the best-looking kid in his school, won all the awards at track and field, and dated the most popular girl." —Anthony Minghella, director of *The Talented Mr. Ripley*

"I'm proud of Matt for handling [stardom] like such a gentleman. He's one of the shining examples of how nice guys can finish first." —Steven Spielberg, director of *Saving Private Ryan*

"I don't think he's very appearance-conscious; he's more about comfort. He's as regular a guy as there is." —Cole Hauser, *School Ties* costar

Matt's Pre-*Will* Work

FILMS	CHARACTER
Chasing Amy (1997)	Executive #2
The Rainmaker (1997; on video May 26, 1998, for rental only)	Rudy Baylor
Glory Daze (1996)	Edgar Pudwhacker
Courage Under Fire (1996)	Specialist Llario
Geronimo: An American Legend (1993)	Lt. Britton Davis
School Ties (1992)	Charlie Dillon
The Good Mother (1988)	(uncredited extra)
Mystic Pizza (1988)	Steamer

TV MOVIES	CHARACTER
The Good Old Boys (1995)	Cotton Calloway
Rising Son (1990)	Charlie Robinson

Other Work

TV commercial for Independent Film Channel (1998)

Matt's Headlines

May 15, 1998: *Entertainment Weekly*.
May 11, 1998: *People*.
May 10, 1998: *Los Angeles Times*.

May 1, 1998: *Entertainment Weekly*.

April 24, 1998: *Entertainment Weekly*.

March 21, 1998: *TV Guide*.

February 28–March 6, 1998: Metro (*The Times,* UK).

February 23, 1998: *People*.

February 13, 1998: *Entertainment Weekly*.

February 1998: *US* magazine.

February 1998: *Written By* magazine.

December 1, 1997: *Newsweek*.

December 1, 1997: *Time*.

December 1997: *Vanity Fair*.

Way-Cool Web Sites

http://members.aol.com/hotdamon/ mattsbio.htm

http://www.silverweb.com/JK/matt.htm
An awesome photo gallery. Page after page of pics. Better than the Damon family album. The quality of the graphics is killer!

http://www.geocities.com/Hollywood/Studio/ 1635/matt.html

http://www.celebsite.com/people/mattdamon/ content/bio.html

http://www.goodmattdamon.com

http://www.mrshowbiz.com/interviews/384_1.html

http://members.aol.com/meliloo/index.html Poetry to the pair

http://www.goodmattdamon.com/planetdamon.html Bills itself as "Planet Damon." One of the all-time-best sites; everything you could want, from quotes to articles to awards. Also, an awesome list of links.

http://www.nexton.com/mdbe/

http://www.pathfinder.com/people/sp/damon/index.html People Online

http://www.excite.com/entertainment/movies/actors_and_actresses/d/matt_damon/

http://www.fansites.com/matt_damon.html

http://www.excite.com/lifestyle/holidays/spring_break/entertainment/celebrities

http://www.digitalhit.com/mattdamon.shtml

http://msn.yahoo.com/Entertainment/Actors_and_Actresses/Damon__Matt/

http://www.x3magazine.com/_goodwil.htm In German

http://www.geocities.com/Hollywood/Studio/1635/

http://members.aol.com/Grlsrock42/mattd.html

http://www.casenet.com/people/
mattdamon.htm

http://www.tv-now.com/stars/mattdam.html
Schedule of Matt's TV appearances

http://members.tripod.com/~lorax/matt.html

http://www.cyberdesic.com/surfers/suzy/
matt/

http://members.aol.com/hotdamon/
mattdamo.htm

http://members.aol.com/PalmTree21/
mattdamon.html

http://members.aol.com/lholmes11/
mdamon.html

http://members.aol.com/FilmCritic/md.html
Matt Damon madness

http://members.aol.com/Cornsilk15/matt.html

http://www.geocities.com/Hollywood/
Bungalow/476 . . .

http://www.geocities.com/Hollywood/
Boulevard/61 . . .

http://members.aol.com/SunsetTea/
MattAndBen.html Both the boys

Movie Sites:

http://www.limbo.com/glorydaze/data/
mattdamon.html *Glory Daze* site

http://movieweb.com/movie/courage/
Courage Under Fire site

http://www.hollywood.com/movies/
rainmaker/ The Rainmaker site.

http://www.therainmaker.com/
The Rainmaker site

http://www.darkhorizons.com/1998/
savingpr/savingn.html Saving Private Ryan
site

http://www.therainmaker.com Talk to me,
Matt, talk to me! The official movie site
includes audio interviews with you-know-
who!

"My character Rudy has a good heart. What
I love about him is he honestly wants the
truth and he's really trying to do what's
right," Matt has said of his *Rainmaker*
character.

Write Matt:
>   c/o CAA
>   9830 Wilshire Blvd.
>   Beverly Hills, CA 90210

Pop Quiz: *Are You a Matt Maven?*

Answer these questions and see if you know
him as well as you think you do.

1. In what movie did Matt act with screen greats Robert Duvall and Gene Hackman?

    (a) *The Rainmaker*

    (b) *The Good Old Boys*

    (c) *Courage Under Fire*

    (d) *Geronimo: An American Legend*

2. What country music star appeared with Matt in *The Rainmaker*?

    (a) Dolly Parton

    (b) Willie Nelson

    (c) Randy Travis

    (d) Reba McEntire

3. What actor directed Matt in *The Good Old Boys*?

    (a) Clint Eastwood

    (b) Tommy Lee Jones

    (c) Robert Redford

    (d) Kevin Costner

4. Where does Matt's mom work?

    (a) MIT

    (b) Harvard

    (c) Lesley College in Cambridge

    (d) Miramax Films

5. What type of watch was Matt spotted wearing while filming *Rounders*?

   (a) Rolex

   (b) Swatch

   (c) Swiss Army

   (d) Timex

Answers: 1. d; 2. c; 3. b; 4. c; 5. c

CHAPTER 5

Big Ben: "Hollywood, Here I Come!"

"It's Aah-ffleck. Like in affluent. Got that?" —Ben

Flash back more than twenty years: A precocious tyke named Ben Affleck announces he's going to be a movie star when he grows up. "My parents totally did not want me to become an actor," he told *Interview*. "I don't think they were thrilled with the prospect of their kid facing a lifetime of rejection and scrapping for a sandwich."

But Ben showed them! With hardly any effort, he nabbed his first TV job at the age of eight—as host, no less, of a PBS educational program. Sure the show was only seen on Boston's Channel 2—but he thought it was his big break and couldn't wait to brag to his bud Matt. "I visited Mayan ruins," he recalls, laughing. "Hey, wasn't it clear that I was Oscar material?"

After several small parts and afterschool specials, Ben finally DID get some meatier parts, playing jocks and bullies ("the kind of guy who'd beat you up") in the films *School Ties* and *Dazed and Confused*.

But in 1993, when a TV series came up, NBC execs still weren't convinced he had star potential. They were less than thrilled with Ben being cast as the lead—the reluctant star quarterback in a small Texas town—in the touchy-feely series *Against the*

Grain. "They didn't really want him," the show's co-creator, Dave Alan Johnson, told *TV Guide.* "But we were sold. We knew he could do it."

The show was short-lived, but Ben didn't lose hope. With equal parts bravado ("I'm a great salesman") and talent, he landed more memorable roles, first in 1995's *Mallrats* (as the store manager obsessed with having his way with Shannen Doherty), and then as the male lead in the 1997 romantic comedy *Chasing Amy* (about a guy who falls for a lesbian). He rounded out the year with *Going All the Way* (as a soul-searching Korean War vet). The timing couldn't have been better—Ben admits he was "one or two *Family Matters* episodes away from flipping burgers."

But now he can put those worries behind him. This summer, he flexes his (enormous!) muscles along with Bruce Willis in the $100 million asteroid extravaganza *Armageddon.* The action flick has blockbuster written all over it: could a Ben Affleck action figure be far behind?

"I'm lovin' it," he admits, boldly. "Look, you want people to look at you and love you and go, 'Oh you're wonderful!'" He pauses to reconsider. "You know, narcissism is the part of my personality I'm least proud of!"

But after all those years of plugging away, who can blame him for boasting? Ben has earned his spot in the Big Time! "There's a part of me that goes, 'Why me?'" he told *US* magazine. "But there's also a part saying, 'Why NOT me?'"

Ben's Bio

Name: Benjamin G. Affleck

DOB: August 15, 1972

Home turf: Born in Berkeley, CA; moved to Cambridge, MA, at a young age.

Height: 6' 2"

Family ties: Ben's mother is a teacher and his dad is a counselor at a drug rehab center in California.

Any more like him at home? Little bro Casey (three years younger than Ben) is also an actor (he played a teen murderer in *To Die For*, a small part in *Chasing Amy*, and Morgan in *Good Will Hunting*—nothing like nepotism!).

School ties: Attended University of Vermont in Burlington; Occidental College in Eagle Rock, CA (in 1992 when he was filming *School Ties*). He later dropped out.

His vices: Camel Lights, Diet Coke, and McDonald's

His appeal: "Ben's far from the jock jerk types he's played. I totally trust him." —Kevin Smith, director of *Mallrats* and *Chasing Amy*

"There's an innocence about Ben and a real strength." —Jerry Bruckheimer, producer of *Armageddon*

Ben's Pre-*Will* Work

FILMS	CHARACTER
Phantoms (January 1998; on video July 14, 1998, for rental only)	Sheriff Bryce Hammond
Going All the Way (1997)	Gunner Casselman
Chasing Amy (1997)	Holden McNeil
Office Killer (1997)	(uncredited)
Glory Daze (1996)	Jack
Mallrats (1995)	Shannon Hamilton
Dazed and Confused (1993)	O'Bannion
School Ties (1992)	Chesty Smith

TV SERIES	CHARACTER
Against the Grain (1993)	Joe Willie Clemons
Almost Home (1993)	Guested as Kevin Johnson in "Is That All There Is?" episode
The Voyage of the Mimi (1984)	C. T. Granville

TV MOVIES	CHARACTER
Danielle Steel's "Daddy" (1991)	Ben Watson
Hands of a Stranger (1987)	Billy Hearn
Lifestories: Families in Crisis (1994)	Aaron Henry

Other Work

Directed a short film titled "I Killed My Lesbian Wife, Hung Her on a Meathook, and Now I Have a Three-Picture Deal at Disney"

Ben's Headlines

June 1998: *Jump* magazine.

May 1998: *YM* magazine.

April 1998: *Seventeen.*

March 2, 1998: *People.*

March 1998: *Teen People.*

March 1998: *Premiere.*

March 1998: *YM.*

February 2, 1998: *People.*

February 13, 1998: *Entertainment Weekly.*

February 1998: *GQ.*

January 30, 1998: *Entertainment Weekly.*

Creative Screenwriting, Volume 5, no. 1, pp. 12–13.

May 1997: *US* magazine.

Way-Cool Web Sites

http://www.worldsite.net/~stef/ben.html
Extensive and impressive—especially the
transcripts of obscure interviews. The movie
reviews are great, too: They said WHAT
about BEN?

http://www.ghgcorp.com/vision/benaffleck/
An amazing compilation of all things Affleck.
Daily gossip and news (the dedication is truly
incredible!) as well as web rings.

http://edge.edge.net/~dphillip/bcaffleck.html
A tribute to the Affleck brothers, including
an on-line look-alike contest. Fab photos—
who can choose between them?

http://www.pond.com/~jshih/ben.html
Need to know every nook and cranny of
Ben's life? Look no further. It's here—the
complete filmography, bio—even Matt
mania! The frequent updates of info on his
new projects are another plus.

http://www.katieweb.com/ben/index.html

*http://www.yahoo.com/Entertainment/
Actors_and_Actresses/Affleck__Ben/*

*http://www.geocities.com/Hollywood/Studio/
9640/*

http://www.expage.com/page/benaffleck

http://members.aol.com/SunsetTea/ MattAndBen.html Double the fun. A site that spotlights both the boys. Includes detailed bios (as if you don't know it all already!).

Write Ben:
> c/o CAA
> 9830 Wilshire Blvd.
> Beverly Hills, CA 90210

The Case on Casey

Ben's baby bro has a big career of his own. He has two new flicks, *200 Cigarettes* and *Desert Blue*, slated for this year. His other credits include:

FILMS	CHARACTER
Good Will Hunting (1997)	Morgan
Chasing Amy (1997)	Little Kid
Race the Sun (1996)	Daniel Webster
To Die For (1995)	Russell Hines

TV MOVIES	CHARACTER
The Kennedys of Massachusetts (1990)	Robert (ages 12–15)
Lemon Sky (1987)	Jerry

Pop Quiz: *The Name Game*

"If I had a dime for every time someone mispronounced my name . . ." laments Ben. Aay-fleck. Ah-fleck. Uh-fleck. Would someone PLEASE get it right! But he should feel better knowing he's not the only one. Pretend you're Rosie or Oprah and introduce these star names. Then check your moniker knowledge below.

1. Charlize Theron
2. Yasmine Bleeth
3. Milla Jovovich
4. Ione Skye
5. Cary Elwes

1. Shar-LEEZ THAIR-on; 2. YAZZ-min Bleeth; 3. MEE-la JOE-vo-vich; 4. Eye-OH-née Sky; 5. CAR-ee EL-ways.

Pop Quiz: *Ben Brainteaser*

1. Besides *Good Will Hunting* and the upcoming *200 Cigarettes*, what other film has Ben appeared in with his little bro, Casey?
    (a) *Office Killer*
    (b) *Chasing Amy*
    (c) *Glory Daze*

(d) *Dazed and Confused*

2. What was *Chasing Amy*'s original title?
   (a) *Comic Strip*
   (b) *Catching Amy*
   (c) *Cat and Mouse*
   (d) *My Name Is Amy*

3. What hit teen TV show is filmed at Ben's alma mater, Occidental College?
   (a) *Dawson's Creek*
   (b) *Saved by the Bell*
   (c) *Beverly Hills, 90210*
   (d) *Boy Meets World*

4. What is Ben's biggest fear?
   (a) spiders
   (b) the dark
   (c) flying
   (d) water

5. What hit movie did Casey turn down a lead role in?
   (a) *Scream 2*
   (b) *Titanic*
   (c) *Armageddon*
   (d) *I Know What You Did Last Summer*

Answers: 1. b; 2. a; 3. c; 4. c; 5. a

CHAPTER 6

Do You Have What It Takes to Be a Hollywood HOTSHOT?

Ben and Matt knew where it was at—they combined integrity and ingenuity with hard work to get to the top. Do you have what it takes to take Tinseltown by storm, too? Sharpen your No. 2s and take this test to find out.

1. You drop by the office of a major studio exec—and are quickly shown the door by his secretary. You:

   (a) Thank the lovely woman and send her a box of Godiva with a note that reads, "Would you be so SWEET as to schedule an appointment with Mr. De Mille?"

   (b) Dress up like a Fed Ex guy and sneak by when she's not looking.

2. A studio is interested in your screenplay—a moving drama about a young janitor genius. Just one prob: They want to turn the tale into a gore-and-guts horror flick titled *Good Will Goes Hunting . . . For Blood!* You:

   (a) Say, "Thanks—but no thanks." You have to be true to your vision.

   (b) Sell, sell, sell! Who cares if your movie stars Neve Campbell as yet another victim? At least this time the killer's a homicidal maniac with a work ethic!

3. Oprah, Dave, and Jay are all asking you to appear on their programs. You:

(a) Jet between New York, Chicago, and L.A.—even if it means no sleep for a week! This is the kind of exposure you've always dreamed of.

(b) Let 'em beg. You're way too big to waste your time. Besides . . . where were they when you needed them?

4. Woody Allen offers you a one-liner (at a tiny salary) in his next movie. You:

(a) Graciously accept—it's an opportunity to learn from a master!

(b) Pass. "Sorry, Wood—I don't work for peanuts!"

5. You've been asked to play a sumo-wrestler-turned-male-dancer in a new indie movie. You:

(a) Politely pass on the part. It doesn't feel right.

(b) Grab it—hey, if these guys are willing to pay you to plump up 100 pounds, why not?

6. The tabloids are trying to make you the

scandal du jour. You:

(a) Shrug it off. It's not true—so why make a bigger deal of it? Besides, tabloid rumors go with the Tinseltown territory!

(b) Sue! Sue! Sue! That's the last time they say they saw you guzzling Slurpees at 7-Eleven at 2 AM!

7. A sleazy agent says he can pull some strings and land you the lead in *Titanic II*. You:

(a) Check him out extensively before signing on the dotted line.

(b) Hire him—he's your kinda guy!

8. A director tells you a scene in your script just isn't working for him. He'd like a rewrite first thing in the AM. You:

(a) Burn the midnight oil to have even more brilliant dialogue on his desk by dawn.

(b) Tell him to go rewrite himself—you don't do unreasonable deadlines.

9. A Hollywood head honcho relays a message through his assistant: "Don't call us—we'll call you." You:

(a) Wait patiently for a few days before calling back with a reminder.

Persistence pays off.

(b) Pester him every hour, on the hour, until he takes your call. No one blows you off!

10. Your motto is:

(a) "If it is to be, it's up to me."

(b) "Don't get mad . . . get millions."

11. A temperamental costar storms off the set claiming he can't work with you. You:

(a) Try and call a truce and work this out.

(b) Insist they can the creep—he was hogging your spotlight anyway.

12. Your alma mater asks you to speak at graduation as a distinguished alumnus. You:

(a) Accept—you're grateful for the support of all your friends and teachers.

(b) Are they kidding? You have three premieres and a *Vanity Fair* interview to do that day!

13. A producer is looking for someone with a lot of experience to play the lead in his new film. You have zippo credits

(unless you count that Trident commercial).
You:

>(a) Tell him you're a hard worker, a quick learner, and you'll give it your all.

>(b) Lie through your teeth. Tell him you were Matt's first choice for the role of Will but you couldn't disappoint Spielberg.

14. You're going to the Oscars. You take as your date:

>(a) Your mom. She's been behind you all the way.

>(b) Sandra, Cameron, Neve, Jewel— any hot movie babe of the moment. You'll look great together on *Entertainment Tonight*.

15. Your best bud calls, begging you to give him a role in your next screenplay. You:

>(a) Talk to the producers and convince them what you already know—your pal is supa-talented and would be an asset to the pic.

>(b) Tell him to find his own movies and stop mooching off of you.

How You Rate

Mostly A's: You have the perfect blend of courage, charisma, and compassion to be a success in this biz. You won't sell out or stoop low; you're willing to pay your dues and give credit to the people who've helped you along the way. You're a nice guy/gal—and just take it from Matt and Ben: Nice guys DO finish first! Hollywood, here you come!

Mostly B's: The world is your doormat—you're willing to walk all over everybody to get to the top. Well, once you're there, you'll find life a little lonely with no friends! Fame and fortune aren't "all that." Can the bravado and no-ethics act, or you'll find yourself a Hollywood has-been in no time at all. Remember, if you're going to burn bridges, you better be a good swimmer. Stick by your old friends, and they'll stick by you.

CHAPTER 7

The Buddy Bond

"The most reassuring thing is that you can look at something and think, 'This is better than if we did it by ourselves.'" —Ben

Laverne & Shirley. Batman and Robin. The Lone Ranger and Tonto. Ben and Matt. These are pals who always stick together, through thick and thin, through breakups and breakdowns. They laugh in the face of long-distance phone bills; they're always available (even in the wee hours of the morning) when duo duty calls.

Is there some magic formula to keeping a friendship superglued? Good will toward others (pun intended) works wonders. Just take it from Los Dos Amigos.

Ben:

"The secret of our friendship? We don't pull any punches with each other."

"Why have we stayed friends? Because we lie for each other in crucial moments."

"We don't fight. We just pout."

"We share a common frame of reference. He'll say something like, 'Remember that time? Glass-eyed Leslie? Let's use that!' It's a kind of familiarity that gives you a certain shorthand. We have a common sense of humor."

Matt:

"It's so much better that [celebrity] happened to both of us at the same time. It makes it more special. To look over and see it happening to your best friend is pretty cool."

"We grew up together, and I think we look at the world the same way. He's the funniest guy I know and the best actor I've ever met. I just admire him greatly."

"I don't care if we're nominated for Best Morons, because I'd think, 'Well, I got nominated with Ben and that's pretty cool.'"

"Ben cheated on me in '87. That was a really dark time. But we don't really fight."

"We're constantly accused of being the most boring people ever. We always wind up at the same bar every night with the same people telling jokes. We've always been that way."

Friend Flicks: *Some Pics to Watch with a Pal*

Beavis & Butt-head Do America (1996): Heh-heh-heh. Gotta love this demented duo.

Wayne's World (1992) and *Wayne's World 2* (1993): A friendship fun fest—you'll laugh, you'll cry, you'll hurl. Party on, Garth!

Bill & Ted's Bogus Journey (1991): A most awesome time-traveling twosome.

Thelma and Louise (1991): These wild women go to the ends of the earth (literally) for each other.

Bill & Ted's Excellent Adventure (1989).

TV Twosomes

Match these pal pairs to their shows.

1. Corey and Sean	a.	*The Wonder Years*
2. Potsie and Ralph	b.	*I Love Lucy*
3. Lenny and Squiggy	c.	*Leave It to Beaver*
4. Eddie and Waldo	d.	*Boy Meets World*
5. Dawson and Joey	e.	*Sabrina, the Teenage Witch*
6. Kelly and Donna	f.	*Happy Days*
7. Kevin and Paul	g.	*Laverne & Shirley*
8. Wally and Eddie	i.	*Family Matters*
9. Ricky and Fred	j.	*Dawson's Creek*
10. Sabrina and Valerie	k.	*Beverly Hills, 90210*

Answers: 1. d; 2. f; 3. g; 4. i; 5. j; 6. k; 7. a; 8. c; 9. b; 10. e.

Pop Quiz: *Are You a Perfect Pal?*

1. Your best bud calls with a crisis: She needs to borrow your cute new crop top for her date with the high school stud. You were planning on wearing it to a party this very night. You:

(a) Hand it over. She's got to dress to impress, and she'd lend you her left arm if you needed it.

(b) Apologize and pass. Hey—you never know who might be at this bash, and you have to look your best.

2. Your close chum has a lit class final tomorrow and is flunking miserably. He asks you if you'll help him cram. Just one prob: Your gal is due over for a date in two hours. You:

(a) Ring Ms. Right and tell her you've come down with a sudden stomach virus.

(b) Lend him your Cliff's Notes collection and enjoy the evening out.

3. Girlfriend just got a hairstyle from hell. She asks you how you like it and you reply:

(a) "It's a whole new you!"

(b) "A paper bag over your head would help."

4. Your friend for life lands the lead in the school play opposite a Matt Damon dead-ringer. You wanted this role so bad you could taste it. You:

(a) Offer your wholehearted congrats and promise to sit front row center on

opening night, cheering her on.
(b) Tell her you'd heard a William Morris agent will be in the audience—no pressure.

5. Your amigo dented his mom's convertible and is asking you to cover for him. You:
(a) Lie through your teeth. "I swear, Mrs. Smith, Marco was with me at the Bowlarama last night."
(b) Fess up to his folks. Why should you take the rap for his recklessness?

How You Rate

Mostly A's. You'd make a heck of an Affleck! You're a bud that's true blue—your friends are lucky to have you!

Mostly B's: Et tu, Brute? You call yourself a compadre? With friends like you, who needs enemies?

CHAPTER 8

The Write Stuff

"The trick to working together is abuse each other. If you can't be honest with the guy, how can it work?"
—Ben

You know that term paper you absolutely dread? The 50-pager you'll spend hours wracking your brain to write? That's how *Good Will* got its start—as a creative writing class assignment for then-Harvard student Matt Damon in 1992.

Sweating to make his prof's deadline, he wrote a one-act tale of a misunderstood young genius and thought that that would be the end of it. But something about the character kept him coming back. "It occurred to me that this guy, this Will Hunting, could have big screen potential," Matt said. "Hey, I wanted to play him! But then I thought, 'You're dreaming, man.'"

So he showed it to his buddy Ben, the one person he thought would understand his aspirations and offer an honest opinion. Ben gave it a once-over, and beamed. This was definitely, he told his pal, a movie-in-the-making! They agreed to work on it as a team—after all, what are friends for?

Though they had acted together in high school plays, collaborating on a script was a whole other story. Where—and how—would they start?

"I think we did it out of frustration and desperation," Matt says. "We couldn't get hired as actors, so we wanted to create work for ourselves. Besides, we had read a lot of scripts, at least five hundred a year. So we thought we'd take a crack at this one ourselves. We just thought it would be fun and interesting to try. We never expected the process to yield such amazing results. I guess you never know."

Nor did the guys know ANYTHING about writing a screenplay—as actors, they were handed a completed script and never got involved in the process. "I was an English major," Matt says. "That was the extent of my writing experience."

At first, they agreed to put it away for a while. But one night, as Matt told Oprah, "we were bored, doing nothing productive, and we just started talking. The script poured out from there." What's the secret of their success? "We don't have one; we were winging it," Matt says. "I think we just used our common sense and our creativity, and that carried us along."

Step 1: *The Brainstorming Session*

Matt and Ben began by letting the ideas flow—and some of them were pretty crazy. *Good Will Hunting* actually started out as a thriller! They improvised each scene together before putting the words down on paper. "Basically, we tried to make each other laugh," Matt says. "It went off in all directions and some of the things we came up with just wound up in the garbage. But some were great and we built on them. The hard part was stringing it all together."

At the time, the pair was rooming together, working "whenever the mood struck us," Matt told *Written By* magazine. "We never forced ourselves. We just sat down haphazardly. There was absolutely no rhyme or reason to it."

Step 2: What Makes Will Tick?

To plot Will's life, they needed to understand him—to get inside his head. "We looked in a few encyclopedias to make ourselves sound more intelligent," Ben adds. "We asked ourselves, 'What if you could read everything rapidly and retain it? What if you could charm the perfect woman?' In our minds, Will was a totally heroic character."

Step 3: Back to the Drawing Board

Just as a scene requires several takes to be captured perfectly on film, a script needs several drafts before it's ready, too. Matt and Ben abandoned their original thriller plot for a sweeter, more sensitive character-driven

"Golden boy" Matt flashes his now-famous,
mega-watt smile . . .

(©1997, Dennis Van Tine/London Features)

... while Ben burns up the camera with his smoldering good looks. All *this* and brains, too. How could two people be so lucky?

(©1997, Kevin Mazur/London Features)

Matt's big break came as a prep school boy in *School Ties*. Can you spot another now-famous prep-pie before he went "wild" and one who later became one-half of a different Dynamic Duo?*

(©1992, Paramount Pictures/Shooting Star)

Rising star Matt Damon pictured here with actor Brian Dennehy in *Rising Sun*.

(©1993, TNT/Shooting Star)

*Answer: Brendan Fraser from *George of the Jungle* sits to Matt's right and Chris O'Donnell of *Batman* fame stands in back of Matt.

Chasing Amy costar Joey Lauren Adams poses here for a publicity shot with Ben.
(©1997, Miramax Films/Shooting Star)

GOOD WILL HUNTING

The poster boys for comedy and drama, Robin Williams and Matt Damon.
(©1997, Miramax Films/Shooting Star)

You can bet these boys won't be benched this season.
(©1997, Miramax Films/Shooting Star)

Boston boys make good! The Cambridge cuties at the New York premiere of *Good Will Hunting*.
(©1997, Dennis Van Tine/London Features)

Ben and Matt arrive for the 1998 Golden Globe Awards with *Good Will Hunting* director, Gus Van Sant. (©1998, P.E.N./ V. Zuffante/Starfile)

Matt and Ben share a Minnie hug.
(©1997, Steve Granitz/Retna)

Ben and his best girl—his proud mom, Chris.
(©1998, Barry King/Shooting Star)

Matt with his happy parents at
the Academy Awards. (©1998,
Gregg De Guire/London Features)

Matt, Ben, and *Good Will* costar Robin Williams
celebrate their crowning achievement—the first
Oscar for all three.
(©1998, Ron Davis/Shooting Star)

Matt practices his poker face on the set of *Rounders* with movie costar Ed Norton.
(©1998, Freddy Baez/UFB/London Features)

Ben chillin' with costar Peter O'Toole in the film *Phantoms*.
(©1998, John P. Johnson/Shooting Star)

drama. "In the end, we saw *Good Will Hunting* as a story about coming of age," Ben says. "It's about making that step from young adulthood to adulthood."

"We used this character as a basis for a story that said something about engaging in life, experiencing it to the fullest, and allowing yourself to be vulnerable to people who you care about," Matt adds. "It's about learning how to be smart in life."

Step 4: Write What You Know

It's the oldest advice in the book: Write from the heart and you can't go wrong. While *Good Will* could have been set in any elite college (why not Yale or even Oxford?), the boys agreed to stick to Matt's original idea of MIT (the Massachusetts Institute of Technology). What Matt and Ben knew and loved best was Boston, the city they had grown up in, and intimate details would make the movie feel real. "We wanted something that captured the essence of our hometown," Ben explains.

With all the pieces in place, what was needed now were the brilliant words to bring Will's hunt to life. Just one small problem: Matt and Ben's careers were taking them in two different directions. While Matt remained in the East for a while before making a cable TV movie in Texas, Ben went West to Hollywood. They relied on the phone, fax, and Fed Ex, and built up the frequent flyer miles over the next two years. "One day, we just looked at what we had done and said, 'Okay. This is it. It's ready,'" Ben says.

And the timing couldn't have been better.

Screenwriting 101

"Hey, if we can do it, anyone can," jokes Ben. Itchin' to ink your own movie?

Read up:

· *American Screenwriters: An Insider's Look at the Art, Craft, and Business of Writing for the Movies* by Karl Schanzer (Avon Books)

· *The Art of Adaptation: Turning Fact and Fiction into Film* by Linda Seger (Henry Holt)

· *The Complete Book of Scriptwriting* by J. Michael Straczynski (Writer's Digest Books)

· *Making a Good Script Great* by Linda Seger (Dodd, Mead & Company)

· *Writing Screenplays That Sell* by Michael Hauge (McGraw-Hill)

Way-Cool Web Sites for Writing Info

http://www.wga.org/ The Writers Guild

http://www.hollywoodnetwork.com:80/hn/ writing/index.html

http://www.teleport.com/~cdeemer/ scrwriter.html

Other Sources to Scout

The Hollywood Scriptwriter Newsletter
1626 N. Wilcox #385
Hollywood, CA 90028
818–991–3096

Script Services

Start by seeing how it was done. Besides, who wouldn't wanna read every word of *Good Will Hunting*? Order it by calling:

Script City
8033 Sunset Blvd., Suite 1500
Hollywood, CA 90046
1–800–676–2522
Fax: (213) 871–9260 (24 hours)
$14.95/script, 4 weeks delivery; add $15 for rush order

Or pick it up in book form:
Good Will Hunting, by Matt Damon, Ben Affleck, and Gus Van Sant (Hyperion, 1997)

Putting It on Paper: Some Tips on Typing Your Masterpiece

CAPS call attention. Use them for:

· CHARACTER NAMES, e.g., "WILL enters the room and SEAN is seated in a chair by the window."

· The words ENTERS and EXITS.

· SOUNDS that make a big noise, e.g., a GUNSHOT or a DOOR SLAMMING.

· SLUGS—tags that signal the scene, telling you where the action is: INT. (for INTERIOR) and EXT. (for EXTERIOR); a specific place, e.g., MIT LECTURE HALL; or a time of day, e.g., SUNRISE, SUNSET.

· TRANSITIONS—phrases that help move the action along. They're followed by a colon, e.g., CUT TO: A hole-in-the-wall college bar; or FADE IN: an abandoned construction site in South Boston.

(Parentheses) provide direction.

· Some examples: SKYLAR (sobbing); WILL (shouting); or SEAN (responding sarcastically).

Pop Quiz: *What's Your* Good Will *Wisdom?*

1. What school is Skylar planning to attend after graduation?
    - (a) Stanford Medical School
    - (b) Syracuse University
    - (c) Oxford
    - (d) Yale

2. What does Skylar say she sees when she looks at a piano?
    - (a) Mozart
    - (b) Chopsticks
    - (c) Billy Joel
    - (d) Beethoven

3. What organization does Will interview with?
    - (a) N.S.A.
    - (b) P.T.A.
    - (c) F.B.I.
    - (d) U.F.T.

4. What does Chuckie bring Will every morning?
    - (a) A bagel with lox and cream cheese
    - (b) A pack of Parliaments
    - (c) A six-pack of Bud
    - (d) A Dunkin' Donuts coffee

5. What type of car do the Southie boys cruise in?

(a) A blue Delta 88
(b) A red Corolla
(c) A black Porsche
(d) A tan Range Rover

Answers: 1. a; 2. b; 3. a; 4. d; 5. a

CHAPTER 9

A Little Good Will
Goes a Long Way

You've heard the Hollywood cliché: "It's not what you know, it's who you know." Luckily, besides brains, Matt and Ben had some great connections in Hollywood. And with a script in hand, it was time to start shmoozing and selling their idea.

They were wise to the industry's game: No matter how great a script is, you need mega bucks to make it. That's where the business side—the agents, producers, and studio execs—came into play. And that's when Matt and Ben discovered a little good will goes a long way!

Just around the time the *Good Will* script was ready, Ben was starring in a flick called *Glory Daze*, which Matt had a small part in as well. He politely asked his movie's producer, Chris Moore, to take a look. Moore was wowed, and started the ball rolling by offering his influence.

"You Call Us . . . Or We'll Call You!"

With more coaxing from the persuasive pair ("we called every friend and colleague we had," Ben admits), the manuscript began circulating around Hollywood. The reaction was overwhelmingly positive. "We felt very lucky that people responded to our work as favorably as they did," Matt says. "It was really exciting for us to hear so much great feedback and feel so much support." The boys found themselves in the center of a studio bidding war: everyone wanted *Good Will*! "We met with a lot of studios who said, 'This is what we'd want to do with it,'" Matt told *Written By* magazine. Castle Rock Entertainment finally landed the rights.

"Here's Ben, sleeping on my couch in a tiny place in West Hollywood, and we suddenly sell our script for half a million. We go from eating Ramen Pride to spaghetti!" Matt told *Mr. Showbiz Online*.

The first thing they did was get some new digs—a bigger house with four bedrooms. "I kept telling Matt to pinch me," Ben jokes. "I thought, 'It couldn't be this easy!'"

If at First You Don't Succeed, Try, Try Again!

Ben was on target: it wasn't THAT easy. Castle Rock requested numerous rewrites, then the film went into Hollywood limbo. But the guys refused to give up hope. They vowed to be patient and plowed ahead with their acting. In 1995, while Ben was working on *Chasing Amy*, he showed *Good Will* to the movie's writer/director Kevin Smith and producer Scott Mosier. Once again, the reaction was "Wow!" They sent the script to Miramax co-chairman Harvey Weinstein.

"I quickly sent Harvey a fax: 'Dear Harvey, I am *The Rainmaker*. I'm that guy.' I was begging." The exec was impressed with Matt's moxie—and loved the script. He in turn sent it to producer Lawrence Bender of *Pulp Fiction* fame.

"When I read the screenplay, I saw immediately that it had great heart," Bender says. This was the break the boys had been waiting for: *Good Will* was finally on its way!

At the same time, Matt and Ben's masterpiece had also caught the eye of director Gus Van Sant—thanks to Ben's little bro, Casey. He had worked with Gus on the 1995 movie *To Die For*, and passed him the script on the set.

"It was probably the best-written screenplay I had ever read," Gus told the *Boston Phoenix*. "I wanted to work on it as soon as I closed the last page. It was wonderful. We called it a color-by-numbers script: if you just filled in the scenes as they were written, it would come to life."

Casting the *Good Will* Gang

Of course they now needed amazing actors

to breathe life into the characters as well. Matt and Ben each assumed the roles they had improvised while writing: Will and his best bud and fellow Southie, Chuckie.

For Sean the psychologist, the pair had always envisioned Robin Williams. And the actor WAS interested. "I saw the story as a battle of wills," Robin says. "Four different parties are vying for Will's soul: a mathematician, a therapist, a girlfriend, and a best friend."

Robin agreed to come on board if they could juggle filming around his very tight schedule: shooting would have to start in five and a half weeks. Talk about a tight prep period! The rest of the principals— Minnie Driver and Stellan Skarsgård—were cast in record time, and it was on to Toronto and Boston to start shooting. There were, of course, a few hitches. Like the time Gus asked the guys to rewrite the movie's ending.

"Gus said, 'I want Chuckie to get flattened on the construction site,'" Matt recalls. "We said 'What do you mean?' He said, 'Killed. Crushed like a bug.' We went, 'No, Gus, that's a terrible idea.' But he made us write it anyway. And when he read it, he said, 'You know, you're right.'"

Turns out, Matt and Ben were right all along—especially about the poignant story's potential and their ability to turn it into a hit movie.

"It was what we were hoping for, dreaming about, but when it actually came to fruition, it was a surprise," Matt admits. "It was like one day, we were joking around, the next day, 'Lights! Camera! Action!' It's sort of surreal. I don't know how Ben and I will ever top it."

Can't wait to see them try!

Role Call

Producers: Be Gentlemen Limited Partnership, Lawrence Bender, Miramax

Director: Gus Van Sant

Cinematographer: Jean-Yves Escoffier

Original music: Danny Elfman

Costume designer: Beatrix Aruna Pasztor

Film editor: Pietro Scalia

Cast (in credits order):

Robin Williams	Sean McGuire
Matt Damon	Will Hunting
Ben Affleck	Chuckie
Minnie Driver	Skylar

Stellan Skarsgård	Gerard Lambeau
Casey Affleck	Morgan
Cole Hauser	Billy
John Mighton	Tom
Rachel Majowski	Krystyn
Colleen McCauley	Cathy

Way-Cool Web Sites for *Good Will*

http://www.miramax.com The official site for the film

http://us.imdb.com/M/title-exact?Good+Will+Hunting+(1997)

http://www.cinema1.com/movies97/goodwillhunting/us.html

Reviews:

http://www.salonmagazine.com/ent/movies/1997/12/05goodwill.html

http://www.film.com/filma/reviews/quickrev.idc?rev=2905

http://www.mrshowbiz.com/reviews/moviereviews/movies/65473.html

http://www.girlsonfilm.com/reviews/goodwill.html

http://www.usatoday.com/life/enter/movies/lef964.htm

http://www.cinema.pgh.pa.us/movie/
reviews?good+will+hunting

If you've been jonesing for another dose of *Good Will Hunting*, the video releases on July 7, 1998, for rental only.

Robin's Résumé

Name: Robin Williams

DOB: July 21, 1951

Birthplace: Chicago, IL

A boy and his toys: He was the only child of a Ford Motors exec and collected 2,000 toy soldiers in his folks' thirty-room mansion growing up.

All in the family: Wife, Marsha Garces Williams, and three kids, Zachary, Zelda, and Cody. Divorced from Valerie Velardi.

School ties: Robin briefly studied poli sci before enrolling at Juilliard to major in theater (Christopher Reeve was a close pal and classmate).

His big break: After graduation, he did stand-up in nightclubs, where he was discovered for the role of the wacky alien Mork from Ork on *Happy Days*. This led to his own series, *Mork & Mindy,* in 1978.

Applause, applause: Nominated for three

Oscars before his *Will* win; he was voted funniest man alive by *Entertainment Weekly* in 1997; he has won three Grammys: one for the audio recording of *Jumanji,* one for *Live at the Met,* and one for the audio recording of *Good Morning, Vietnam.*

What he loves: Kids and comedy.

What he hates: Following a script. "You gotta just let him run with it, sometimes," says Matt.

Best buds: Whoopi Goldberg and Billy Crystal; the late John Belushi.

Up and coming: *Jakob the Liar*, about a man who shelters a little girl in Nazi Germany; *What Dreams May Come*, the story of a dead man who searches for his wife in the afterlife; *The Interpeter*, about a man who mediates an international crisis; and *Damien of Molokai*, the true story of a priest who tends to a leper colony.

Robin's Pre-*Will* Work

FILM	CHARACTER
Flubber (1997)	Prof. Philip Brainard
Fathers' Day (1997)	Dale Putley
Deconstructing Harry (1997)	Mel

Hamlet (1996)	Osric
Jack (1996)	Jack Powell
The Birdcage (1996)	Armand Goldman
Jumanji (1995)	Alan Parrish
Nine Months (1995)	Dr. Kosevich
To Wong Foo, Thanks for Everything! Julie Newmar (1995)	John Jacob Jingleheimer Schmidt
Being Human (1993)	Hector
Mrs. Doubtfire (1993)	Daniel Hillard/Mrs. Doubtfire
Toys (1992)	Leslie Zevo
Aladdin (1992)	Voice of the Genie
Hook (1991)	Peter Banning/ Peter Pan
The Fisher King (1991)	Parry
Dead Again (1991)	Dr. Cozy Carlisle
Cadillac Man (1990)	Joey O'Brien
Awakenings (1990)	Dr. Malcolm Sayer
Dead Poets Society (1989)	John Keating
Good Morning, Vietnam (1987)	Adrian Cronauer
Club Paradise (1986)	Jack Moniker
The Best of Times (1986)	Jack Dundee
Seize the Day (1986)	Tommy Wilhelm
Moscow on the Hudson (1984)	Vladimir Ivanoff
The Survivors (1983)	Donald Quinelle
The World According to Garp (1982)	T. S. Garp
Popeye (1980)	Popeye

Way-Cool Web Sites for Robin

http://www.yahooligans.com/content/webceleb/williams/
http://www.zdnet.com/yil/content/mag/9702/robin/rw-main.html

The Skinny on Minnie

Name: Amelia "Minnie" Driver

DOB: January 31, 1971

Her hood: England

Her hobbies: Singing and strumming the guitar

School ties: Attended Bedales School in Petersfield, England, and the Webber-Douglas Academy of Dramatic Art in London; majored in drama.

Other boy toys (besides Matt): Taylor Hawkins (musician); Elliott Smith (musician); and Rufus Sewell (actor).

Minnie's Pre-*Will* Work

FILM	CHARACTER
Grosse Point Blank (1997)	Debi Newberry
Sleepers (1996)	Carol
Baggage (1996)	
Big Night (1996)	Phyllis
Golden Eye (1995)	Irina

Circle of Friends (1995)	Benny
The Politician's Wife (1995)	Jennifer Caird
(TV mini-series)	
That Sunday (1994) (TV)	Rachel
Mr. Wroes Virgins (1993)	
(TV series)	
God on the Rocks (1990; TV)	Lydia

*Post-*Will *work: The Governess* (late 1998), a period drama about England's first female professional photographer. Rosina de Silva is a young Jewish nineteenth-century woman who is forced to conceal her identity and take a job caring for a family in Scotland; *Tarzan* (1999), the new Walt Disney animated flick for which Tony Goldwyn is the voice of jungle boy and Minnie's the voice of Jane; *At Sachem Farm* (1999), costarring Nigel Hawthorne (who's also with Miss Minnie in *Tarzan*).

Way-Cool Web Sites for Minnie

*http://www.yahoo.com/Entertainment/
Actors_and_Actresses/Driver__Minnie/*

*http://us.imdb.com/M/person-exact/
Driver,+Minnie*

http://www.bowdish.com/Minnie/minnie.html

*http://www.CelebSite.com/people/
minniedriver/index.html*

*http://www.spe.sony.com/classics/attractions/
governess.html* Info on her new flick

Pop Quiz: *What's Your* Will *Power?*

A brain-busting quiz (yes, it counts!):

1. About how much moolah did *Good Will*
   rake in its opening weekend in the U.S.?
   - (a) $2 million
   - (b) $200,000
   - (c) $20,000
   - (d) $2,000

2. Who wrote the two tunes "Miss Misery"
   and "Morning After" on the movie
   soundtrack?
   - (a) Luscious Jackson
   - (b) Ben Affleck
   - (c) Elliott Smith
   - (d) Al Green

3. International moviegoers from what
   country were the first after the U.S. to
   see *Good Will*?
   - (a) Switzerland
   - (b) Iceland
   - (c) England
   - (d) Canada

4. What type of mathematical equation
   does Will solve on the blackboard?
   - (a) geometry

    (b) physics
    (c) combinatorics
    (d) linear algebra

5. "His mind kicks into super-charged mode—a mere mortal can't keep up." Who was Matt Damon describing?
    (a) Robin Williams
    (b) Gus Van Sant
    (c) His character, Will
    (d) Ben Affleck

6. Who actually created the painting of the rowboat on a stormy sea that hangs in Sean's office?
    (a) Matt Damon
    (b) Ben Affleck
    (c) Gus Van Sant
    (d) Minnie Driver

7. Where did Matt and Ben tell Oprah they went to celebrate the sale of their script?
    (a) New York, for a weekend of wild partying
    (b) The exclusive Viper Room in L.A.
    (c) Melrose Ave., for a mega shopping spree
    (d) Sizzler, for $6.99 all-you-can-eat shrimp

8. How many minutes does the movie run?
    (a) 140
    (b) 125

    (c) 250

    (d) 98

9. What fave hangout of Matt and Ben's was actually used as a location in the movie?

    (a) Woody's L Street Tavern

    (b) The Bronx Zoo

    (c) Burger King

    (d) Kinko's

10. What campus doubled for MIT and Harvard in the movie?

    (a) Columbia University

    (b) George Washington University

    (c) University of Toronto

    (d) Syracuse University

Answers: 1. b; 2. c; 3. d; 4. c; 5. a; 6. c; 7. d; 8. b; 9. a; 10. d

How You Rate

8–10 correct: Mensa material! You could match wits with Will any day.

5–7 correct: B+ student. Here's your homework assignment: Watch *Good Will* a few more times till you sharpen your Southie smarts.

2–4 correct: D student. Detention for you: Write "Matt and Ben rule" 1,000 times.

1 or less correct: A total *Good Will*

wipeout! You're hereby ordered to read this book from cover to cover and write a 50-page report (and don't say that your dog ate it!).

The Inside Track: *Where to Turn . . . What to Say . . . How to Sell Your First Screenplay*

· Hollywood Creative Directory, a guide to studios, networks, production companies, and their staffs. Address: 300 Olympic Blvd., Santa Monica, CA 90404–5041; 310–315–4815 or 800–815–0503.

· *Selling Your Screenplay* by Cynthia Whitcomb (Crown Publishers)

· *How to Sell Your Idea to Hollywood* by Robert Kosberg (HarperCollins)

Sources for addresses, competitions, and tips on how to get your script seen:

http://gladstone.uoregon.edu/~miholer/

http://www.teleport.com/~cdeemer/ tip-home.html

http://www.screenwriters.com/screennet.html

http://www.k-net.net/~hsws/

http://www.geocities.com/Hollywood/4486/

http://TheInkwell.com/

http://www.moviebytes.com

Cinema-Speak

bit: A small, unimportant role, usually lasting only one scene.

call sheet: A listing of which actors will be required for which scenes, and when they will be required.

cameo: A bit part played by a famous actor.

CU: Abbreviation for "close-up."

dailies: Also known as "rushes," these are prints made from the negatives photographed on the previous day. During filming, the director and some actors check out the dailies to rate the progress of the pic.

dope sheet: A list of scenes from the script that have already been filmed.

hot set: A set on which a scene is in the process of being shot. Translation: DO NOT DISTURB!

hype: Buzz, big time. Either through media, word of mouth, or advertising.

ink: To sign a contract or deal.

kickoff: The start of filming and production.

legs: If a movie has 'em, it means it's continuing to bring in big box-office receipts.

majors: The big studios, including MGM/UA, 20th Century Fox, Sony Pictures, Warner Bros., Paramount Pictures, Universal, and Disney.

outtake: A scene not seen in the final print of the film.

ozoner: Slang for drive-in theater.

rhubarb: Background conversation. Historically, when a script called for murmuring, the extras would be required to mumble the word "rhubarb" to create the effect.

A Who's Who of the Crew

Foley artist: The expert who creates extra sound effects (such as footsteps) in a studio, after the scene has been shot.

gaffer: The chief lighting technician.

grip: The guy who handles the production equipment on the set (including the dollies).

helmer: The dude "at the helm," the director.

scout: The person who looks for cool locations to film.

talent: The actors and actresses.

CHAPTER 10

Campus Confidential

When you think Cambridge, two things probably come to mind: Harvard Square and the two schools that are home to every brainiac in the nation. Okay—Harvard and MIT are not exactly schools for slackers. But that doesn't mean these students spend every waking moment discussing the theory of relativity.

"The image people have of us is nerds who walk around with pen protectors in our pockets," complains one MIT freshman. Well, here's a news flash, folks: These people KNOW how to party. Cambridge is one of the coolest college towns in the country. Just ask the boys:

"Cambridge is great. It's not that big of a town," Matt says. "It's like the People's Republic of Cambridge. People stick together there."

Traditionally, movies haven't done the city justice. "They've been populated by people who just don't get it," says Matt. "That bothered us, having grown up there. We knew the worldview, the attitude."

MIT History

Will was in good hands here. A few facts:

· Since it's a mouthful to say "The Massachusetts Institute of Technology," everyone calls it MIT—no periods between the letters, by the way.

· The school's first students were admitted in 1865.

· Charles Marstiller Vest has been the prez since 1990.

· "Education and research—with relevance to the practical world as a guiding principle" is MIT's primary purpose.

· MIT consists of five schools and twenty-one academic departments. It's located on more than 150 acres stretching a mile along the Cambridge side of the Charles River.

· Some fun courses: Chemical Oceanography, Genome Research, Wavelets and Filter Banks, Parallel Scientific Computing, Intro to Microlocal Analysis, Integral Equations and Stochastic Processes. (What, no Wine Tasting or Basket Weaving 101?)

· Within the last five years, research teams at MIT have located the gene defect responsible for a form of muscular dystrophy, fabricated a single-electron transistor, and developed a new optical technique to measure galaxy distances. And that was all before lunch.

· How do you get in? Well, 1,600 on the

SATs and straight A's in high school couldn't hurt. Brains like Will's would work in your favor, too. Last year, about 8,000 kids applied—1,938 were offered admission. If you can figure out that percentage (it's 24%), you might make the waiting list.

· Eleven members of the faculty are Nobel laureates. No pressure, though.

· Matt's connection: "My sister-in-law is a graphic designer for MIT, and she told me how they have chalkboards in the hallways. If you suddenly figure out the key to cold fusion you can just write it there as you're walking to class. That gave me the idea to make Will a janitor who sees the board as he's sweeping up."

· For more info: Write to MIT, 77 Massachusetts Ave., Cambridge, MA 02139–4307; phone: 617–253–1000.

The Hot Spots

Where do Ben and Matt (and anyone with an iota of coolness) hang when they're back in their hometown?

HARVARD YARD: It's the hub of the university. A big knolly green where commencement is held every year and students laze away their days.

CAMBRIDGE COMMON, AKA THE COMMONS: Used to be a grazing pasture—come to think of it, it still is for students! A big park near Harvard Square where you can stroll.

THE CHARLES RIVER: Watch the crew teams row-row-row their boats, or go biking along its banks.

NEWBURY STREET: Boston's answer to Rodeo Drive. Pricey boutiques and the coolest clothing stores (Banana Republic, Gap, Diesel), plus a four-story Tower Records that rocks. Where all the students shop till they drop.

THE COOP: A group of stores and restaurants on the Harvard campus where kids often congregate. The street show ain't bad either: sidewalk musicians, magicians, and cheap-o souvenirs.

CAMBRIDGE RINDGE AND LATIN SCHOOL: Matt and Ben's dear old alma mater, right next-door to Harvard.

REGINA'S PIZZA: In the North End of Boston (the city's answer to Little Italy) for awesome slices with the works.

THE BULL & FINCH: Aka Cheers. You can bet everyone here knows Ben and Matt's names! Touristy—but fun.

Hey . . . That Bar Looks Familiar!

Boston filming locations for *Good Will Hunting*:

MIT campus, Cambridge

Bunker Hill Community College, Boston

Dunster House, Harvard University, Cambridge

Public Garden, Boston

Bow & Arrow Pub, Harvard Square, Cambridge

The Tasty, Harvard Square, Cambridge

Woody's L Street Tavern, Boston

Getting Around

Take "The T," Boston's subway system.

Can We Talk?

"No one has ever accurately portrayed a Boston accent, much less the cultural aspect of the city," says Matt. "You've got to be from there to do it. I don't think even Meryl Streep could do it."

Wanna give it a whirl? Drawl your a's, letting them roll like butta off your tongue. Lock your jaw, think like a Kennedy, and repeat after me:

"Pack-the-caah-in-Hah-vud-yahd."

"Jenni-fuh, I can't see in the daahk."

Way-Cool Web Sites

http://staff.motiv.co.uk/carnold/boston/
A guide to Beantown's best

http://www.TheInsider.com/boston/

http://www.boston.com/

http://boston.sidewalk.com/

http://www.citybuzz.com

http://web.mit.edu/ MIT's school site

CHAPTER 11

Hollywood Heartbreakers

"Everyone screams, 'It's Matt! It's Ben! He's so hot!'" —Robin Williams

One would hardly accuse Matt and Ben of being wallflowers: this pair loves 'em then leaves 'em begging for more! Over the years, their list of ladies has grown steadily—models, movie stars. But not one has been Ms. Right . . . yet. Hey guys—if you're tired of those rich and famous females, give an ordinary girl a try!

Was it always this way? Not exactly . . .

"The girl I took to my prom hooked up with another guy there," Matt told *Teen*. "I was even in the room—hopelessly in love, crying myself to sleep. I mean totally heartbroken, crestfallen."

Pull-eez! Ben protests: "He's always been the one who got all the attention. I was a total failure; it was a catastrophe."

Ben's always been less lucky at love. He was engaged once but broke it off. "Almost every relationship I've ever been in has basically been a train wreck," Ben told *US* magazine. "I have enough trouble maintaining the even keel in the confines of a normal relationship. I don't expect that to get any easier now that everyone wants a piece of me."

But girlfriends, beware: How do these two come up with convincing female characters (like Skylar) for their movies?

"We write down stuff girlfriends have said to us and stuff that has actually happened."

Matt's Amours

He dated model Kara Sands (a real cutie) before falling head-over-heels for his *Rainmaker* costar Claire Danes. They were an item as long as the cameras rolled, even posing as a pair for the paparazzi at the movie's premiere. But alas, their relationship ended shortly thereafter. A year later, in walked Minnie Driver, cast as a sassy Harvard senior who steals Will's heart . . . and soon Matt's.

Once again, Mr. Damon was dazzled: "She read for the part, and she's standing there with this Cheshire cat smile, thinking, 'Would you like to join me in the scene, or are you gonna stand there with your tongue hanging out?' I was all dorky and stuff."

But the flames fizzled shortly before Oscar night. "I was with Minnie for a while, but we're not romantically involved any-more," he says. "We're just really good friends. I love her dearly. I care about her a lot; we care about each other. We just decided it wasn't meant to be, and if it's not meant to be, it's not meant to be." Since then, Minnie has been seen with musician Elliott Smith, actor Rufus Sewell, and Foo Fighters drummer Taylor Hawkins. (For the skinny on Minnie, see page 73.)

So who's new for Matt? How about Claire's *Little Women* costar (and buddy!) Winona Ryder? The pair have been seen around the town, having cozy tête-à-têtes over candlelit dinners. And guess what? They have no plans to make a flick together! This one could be a keeper!

Ben's Babes

He was linked for a long time with Cheyenne Rothman, a girl he's known since high school. But after years of being on again/off-again, he set his sights on someone new. Who? None other than gorgeous Gwyneth (Brad who?) Paltrow, who just happens to be good gal pals with Winona Ryder (Ben and Gwyn; Matt and Noni—how's THAT for a dream double date?). Gwyn and Matt are making *The Talented Mr. Ripley* together (a good reason for Ben to visit his bud on the set), and now rumor has it that Ben's been signed to costar alongside his lady in *Shakespeare in Love*. They've been out and about, taking in some Broadway theater (her mom, Blythe Danner, was recently in a play,

The Deep Blue Sea) and trendy restaurants
(Balthazar on Spring Street), and they plan
to escort each other to openings of his
Armageddon and her *Perfect Murder*. When
reporters ask if they're an item, Ben just
shrugs. Gotta love a man of mystery!

All the Girls They've Loved Before

Wanna know more about Ben and Matt's
main squeezes? Perhaps a clue or two to the
attraction might help YOU see some action
(a girl can dream, can't she?).

Claire's Case History

Name: Claire Catherine Danes

DOB: April 12, 1979

Place of birth: New York City

School ties: Acting classes at Lee
Strasberg since she was nine; completed
high school diploma with tutor; deferred
enrollment to Yale.

All in the family: Father Chris is a
computer consultant; mother Carla is an
artist; older bro Asa is a college senior.

Her hood: Santa Monica, CA

Her hobbies: Gymnastics, dance, surfing,
cruising the freeways in her Chevy Blazer.

Love of her life (no, not Matt!): Her kitty,

Fifi-Champion.

Main man: Dating (on-again/off-again) musician Ben Lee.

Upcoming projects: *Brokedown Palace* (1998), a drug-smuggling drama with Kate Beckinsale, Amanda De Cadenet, Lou Diamond Phillips, and Bill Pullman; *The Mod Squad* (1998), a remake of the TV classic costarring Josh Brolin; *Monterey Pop* (1998) with Ethan Hawke; *Star Quality* (1999), a romantic comedy with Maxwell Caulfield and Michelle Pfeiffer.

Way-Cool Web Sites for Claire

http://cheats.simplenet.com/starlets/claire/claire.html

http://www.geocities.com/Hollywood/3542/claire.html

http://www.tonytang.com/claire/photoalbum

http://us.imdb.com/Name?Danes,+Claire

The Word on Winona

Name: Winona Laura Horowitz

DOB: October 29, 1971

Place of birth: Winona, MN

School ties: Petaluma (California) High School (graduated with a 4.0 average);

American Conservatory Theatre, San Francisco

Family ties: She grew up on a ranch commune in Northern California that had no electricity. She is the goddaughter of Timothy Leary, and her parents were friends of Beat poet Allen Ginsberg.

Former fiancé: Johnny Depp; she also dated David Duchovny.

A natural blond: Her real hair color is how it appeared in *Edward Scissorhands*.

Upcoming projects: *Celebrity* (late 1998), the new Woody Allen opus; *Just to Be Together* (1998) reunites her with Johnny Depp in a romantic drama. Jack Nicholson is rumored to be directing, and Andy Garcia and Sam Shepard costar.

Way-Cool Web Sites for Winona

http://www.geocities.com/Hollywood/Hills/5260/winona.htm#bio

http://www.CelebSite.com/people/winonaryder/index.html

http://us.imdb.com/NUrls?Ryder,+Winona

The Goods on Gwyneth

Name: Gwyneth Paltrow

DOB: September 27, 1972

Place of birth: Los Angeles, CA

School ties: Attended University of California at Santa Barbara

All in the family: Mom and Dad, Blythe Danner and Bruce Paltrow, are both in the biz. She has a brother, Jake.

Se habla Espanol? Si! After spending a time in her early teens in Talavera de la Reina, Spain, she can speak fluent Spanish.

Former fiancé: Brad Pitt

Supa-model: February 1998 *Premiere* cover and December 1997 *Harper's Bazaar* cover.

Upcoming projects: *Shakespeare in Love* (1998), a historical biopic about the bard and Queen Liz, costarring Judi Dench and Gwyn's real-life Romeo, Ben; *The Talented Mr. Ripley* (1999) opposite Matt (she plays Marge).

Way-Cool Web Sites for Gwyneth

http://www.bomis.com/rings/paltrow/

http://www.celebs.net/GwynethPaltrow/gphome.html

http://www.filmscouts.com/people/gwy-pal.html

CHAPTER 12

The Big Night

How's this for an adrenaline rush: From the minute you set foot out of the limo and onto that red carpet outside Hollywood's Shrine Auditorium, there's one thought racing through your head:

"My life may change forever in the next three hours."

The Oscars can make you, or they can break you. That "golden dude," as Robin Williams dubbed him, says you're a star—a mover, a shaker, a box-office blockbuster maker. And along with all the congrats comes the cash: when you're a winner, studios beg to buy your next screenplay. Every director in Hollywood wants to work with you; every time the press refers to you, "Academy Award winner" goes before your first name.

Getting Glam

Think actresses are the only ones to stress over their Oscar attire? Matt and Ben must have tried on a dozen tuxes before deciding on a couple of classic (and pricey!) Armanis. Shoes (supa-shiny) along with elegant cufflinks and studs pull it all together. Of course, men have it a little easier—most women spend the whole day getting primped and powdered, from head (elegant upsweeps) to toe (perfect pedicures). And there's the matter of the ultimate accessories—diamonds from Harry Winston, but of course! Ben's beauty routine: "I shaved."

Thanks, Mom!

While every eligible woman in Tinseltown would have given her right arm to be with the boys this evening, they were loyal to the ladies who've stood by them through thick and thin. "Our dates were our mothers," Ben declared backstage, proudly. "It's nice for our moms to see all this stuff; mine even came to the rehearsal and took pictures. She's considering [Oscar] her grandson, and she's holding it for ransom until she gets her real one."

The Envelope, Please

This is the tensest moment of any nominee's night. You hold your breath, hoping and praying that the name the presenter reads is yours. The cameras close in on your face to get your reaction (total glee or agonizing disappointment). Your name is announced to thunderous applause and you make your way down the aisle to the podium (it seems like a mile away!). Careful not to trip climbing those stairs (hey, it's been done before!).

Smart nominees come prepared: they've either memorized an acceptance speech (just in case!) or carry crib notes. In all the excitement, you're bound to forget to thank somebody (some winners are so psyched they can hardly remember their own names!). What's it like to be a winner? Robin Williams explained: "I've been here three times before and lost," he joked. "Basically my odds before were the same as a Jamaican bobsled team winning. And tonight it was kind of interesting, because I didn't think I had a chance, but when they said it, it was truly a shock, and it's a great honor. I'm sailing. Much cheaper than Prozac."

Meet the Press

So you're swept offstage—you can relax, now, right? WRONG! That's when the fun begins. You're greeted by a mob of reporters from all over the world, asking you how it feels to be The Chosen One. Of course, the only thing you want to do is sneak back to your seat in Shrine Auditorium and bask in the afterglow—fat chance! Clutching your statuette, you pose for endless pictures and give witty and wonderful sound bites. Sure, you're still dazed and confused—just smile and say "CHEESE!"

The Oscar Acceptance Speech

There are two camps when it comes to Oscar oratories: those who keep it short, sweet, and to the point . . . and those who don't. If, like Sally Field, you want audiences to "really, really like you," you say what you have to in seconds and exit, stage left, before the Oscar orchestra begins to drown you out with the theme song from *The Godfather* (how's THAT for a hint?).

When Ben handled the honors, he was sure to get in all the gratitude in under two minutes (I know, I clocked it!). Who'd he thank? Harvey Weinstein and John Gordon from Miramax, Gus Van Sant, Robin Williams, Minnie Driver, his brother Casey ("who's brilliant in the movie,"), Cole Hauser, his mother, Matt's mother, Chris Moore (his agent,), Cuba Gooding, Jr. ("for showing us how to give our acceptance speech"), and "all our friends and family and everybody back in Boston—the whole city of Boston!"

Who didn't he thank? The heavens above, his grammar school teachers, Matt (!), his girlfriend Gwynnie, Armani for supplying his tux. "God, I know we're forgetting somebody!" he said, elbowing Matt.

"Whoever, we forgot, we love you and thank you. Thank you thank you so much!"

De nada, dude!

Couldn't snag an invite to the hottest spot on Oscar night? We'll give you a gander inside . . .

The *Vanity Fair* Fete

What: The annual Oscar party to top all parties, sponsored by the celeb bible, *Vanity Fair* magazine.

Style: Black tie. BYOP (bring your own paparazzi).

Where: Morton's restaurant in West Hollywood.

Who: Anyone who's anyone. The guest list this year included Matt, Ben, their families, Minnie, Kate Winslet, Robin Williams, Winona Ryder, Neve Campbell, Ahnold and Maria, and Madonna.

The menu: Champagne, caviar, and those cute little gourmet mini pizzas. The cuisine is classic American/continental. If you're famous, they'll make you anything you want (rumor has it that Ben asked for a burger!).

Plan on: Dancing till dawn, rubbing elbows with the elite, being asked (way too many times) what your next film is (fake it!), and who designed your dress ("Vera

Wang, dahling . . . ").

Arrive: By limo, fashionably late, of course.

Can you crash? Not a chance. Joe Bouncer at the door wants to see ID—even if you're Leonardo DiCaprio!

Who makes the list: All the major Hollywood players, nominees, anyone who's graced the pages of *Vanity Fair.*

Way-Cool Web Sites for Oscar

http://www.oscar.com

http://www.hollywood.com

http://us.imdb.org/Movies/Oscars/

http://www.chicago.tribune.com/leisure/ movies/siskel98/iphotos.frm A photo gallery

http://www.yahoo.com/Entertainment/Movies _and_Film/Awards/Academy_Awards/History/

Applause, Applause! *Good Will*'s Winning Streak

Academy Awards, 1998:

Best Writing, Screenplay, Written Directly for the Screen: Ben Affleck and Matt Damon

Best Supporting Actor: Robin Williams

Academy Award Nominations for:

Best Actor: Matt Damon

Best Director: Gus Van Sant

Best Film Editing: Pietro Scalia

Best Music, Original Dramatic Score: Danny Elfman

Best Music, Original Song: Elliott Smith, "Miss Misery"

Best Picture

Best Supporting Actress: Minnie Driver

Other Awards:

Golden Globe, 1998, Best Screenplay— Motion Picture: *Good Will Hunting*

Berlin International Film Festival, 1998, Silver Berlin Bear, Outstanding Single Achievement: Matt Damon, for his screen-writing and acting in the film

Boston Society of Film Critics Awards, 1997

3rd place, BSFC Award, Best Screenplay: Ben Affleck and Matt Damon

Broadcast Film Critics Association Awards, 1998, Best Screenplay: Ben Affleck and Matt Damon; Breakout Artist: Matt Damon

Florida Film Critics Circle Awards, 1998, Newcomers of the Year: Ben Affleck and Matt Damon

Golden Satellite Awards, 1998, Best Motion

Picture Screenplay—Original: Ben Affleck and Matt Damon

National Board of Review, USA, 1997, Special Achievement in Filmmaking: Ben Affleck and Matt Damon

Screen Actors Guild Awards, 1998, Outstanding Performance by a Male Actor in a Supporting Role: Robin Williams

Pop Quiz: *And We'd Like to Thank . . .*

Can you identify these folks Matt and Ben often acknowledge?

1. Anthony Kubiak	a. math consultant on the movie
2. Harvey Weinstein	b. Matt's acting teacher
3. David Wheeler	c. Miramax head honcho who was wowed by *Good Will* script
4. Patrick O'Donnell	d. Harvard teacher; Matt wrote early version of *Good Will* in his class.
5. Gerry Speca	e. Matt and Ben's high school drama teacher

Answers: 1. d; 2. c; 3. b; 4. a; 5. e

CHAPTER 13

Coming Attractions

"Topping this? It won't be easy."
—Matt

But if we know Ben and Matt, *Good Will* was only a warm-up. The pair have been bombarded with offers, everything from movies to TV to commercial endorsements. They've been picky with their acting projects, and plan to team again as writers on several future flicks (could there be a *Good Will* sequel in the works?).

"Not only are we going to write together again, we have to," joked Matt backstage Oscar night. "We're contracted to do three more." But in the meantime, they'll be keeping busy.

Matt's Movies

Saving Private Ryan

Release date: July 24, 1998

Director: Steven Spielberg

Studio: Paramount Pictures

CAST:

Matt Damon

Edward Burns

Tom Sizemore

Tom Hanks

The inside scoop: Matt plays the title role in this World War II epic. "It's about these four brothers," he told *Hollywood Online*. "Three of them die in one week beginning with D-Day. There's one surviving brother—that's Private Ryan, my character—behind enemy lines. The movie is about Tom Hanks and a group of hand-picked rangers who are going back to find this guy on essentially a political mission because the government does not want this fourth brother to die. Private Ryan eventually stands for everyone's chance to go home." Matt also said, "He stands for everybody's brother. . . . His character is more important than his characteristics."

Rounders

Release date: September 11, 1998

Director: John Dahl

Studio: Miramax Films

CAST:

Matt Damon

Ed Norton

John Malkovich

John Turturro

Martin Landau

Gretchen Mol

The inside scoop: Matt plays Mike McDermott, a reformed card shark who comes out of retirement to help his ex-con pal pay off a debt. There are some pretty high stakes here: Mike must give up law school, a girlfriend, and the straight-and-narrow path, to rescue a bud. Think he'd do that for Ben?

All the Pretty Horses

Director: Billy Bob Thornton

Studio: Columbia Pictures / Miramax Films

CAST:

Matt Damon

Billy Bob Thornton

The inside scoop: Matt reportedly beat out Leonardo DiCaprio (and nabbed $5.5 million) for this role of a Texan who rides into Mexico in 1949 and falls for a wealthy ranch owner's daughter. The cowboy gets corralled: Daddy has him thrown in prison. But you know our hero triumphs in the end. The industry buzz is that Leo was too big for his britches, asking $15 million to star in this screen adaptation of the best-selling Cormac McCarthy novel. Matt's rumored costars are fifteen-year-old *Sling Blade* star Lucas Black and Penelope Cruz, the Spanish actress who just wrapped up a Western with Woody Harrelson. Matt plans to lose weight (à la *Courage Under Fire*) for the role.

Planet Ice

Release date: Late 1998/early 1999 (currently in production)

Director: Art Vitello

Studio: 20th Century Fox / Fox Animation Studios

CAST:

Matt Damon

Hank Azaria

Drew Barrymore

Jim Breuer

Nathan Lane

Lena Olin

Bill Pullman

The inside scoop: Matt lent his voice to the character Cale in this animated flick. Cale is a nineteen-year-old dude who finds a map and must rescue humanity. No problem!

The Talented Mr. Ripley

Release date: Late 1999 (currently in pre-production)

Director: Anthony Minghella

Studio: Miramax Films / Paramount Pictures

CAST:

Matt Damon

Gwyneth Paltrow

Jude Law

Cate Blanchett

The inside scoop: This remake of *Purple Noon* has been filming on location in romantic Italy with Gwyneth Paltrow. It's a thriller set in 1958 about a young man (Matt) who is sent to Italy by an American businessman to retrieve the businessman's son and bring him back to the U.S. so he can take over the family business. Still with us? Matt's character becomes intrigued by the way of life in Italy so he kills the son and assumes his identity.

Matt had this to say about the movie: "The character is fascinating. It's certainly the most unconventional in terms of movies I've done. The guy goes and falls in love with this man and his life—to the point where he wants to be in his skin."

How he differs from the character: "I'm more beer, and he's more delicate."

Training Day

Release date: 1999

CAST:

Matt Damon

Samuel L. Jackson

The inside scoop: Mum's the word. Sam's producing this pic and specifically wanted Matt.

Ben on the Big Screen

Armegeddon

Release date: July 1, 1998

Director: Michael Bay

Studio: Touchstone Pictures

CAST:

Ben Affleck

Bruce Willis

Billy Bob Thornton

Liv Tyler

The inside scoop: The sky is falling. An asteroid the size of Texas is about to collide with the Earth. Willis and his team (including buddy Ben as A. J. Frost) vow to stop it in its tracks.

200 Cigarettes

Release date: Late 1998 (currently in production)

Director: Risa Bramon Garcia

Studio: MTV/Paramount

Written by Shana Larsen

CAST:

Ben Affleck

Casey Affleck

David Chappelle

Guillermo Díaz

Janeane Garofalo

Gaby Hoffmann

Kate Hudson

Christina Ricci

The inside scoop: New Year's Eve 1982 in the lives of two Long Island girls. Ben is a bartender.

Forces of Nature

Release date: 1999

Director: Bronwen Hughes

Studio: DreamWorks SKG

CAST:

Ben Affleck

Sandra Bullock

Maura Tierney

The inside scoop: Hush-hush, but we hear it's a romantic comedy.

And Matt and Ben, Together Again

Dogma

Release date: Late 1998/early 1999 (currently in production)

Director: Kevin Smith

Studio: Miramax Films

CAST:

Ben Affleck

Matt Damon

Linda Fiorentino

George Carlin

Bud Cort

Dwight Ewell

Janeane Garofalo

Salma Hayek

Jason Lee

Alanis Morissette (as God)

Alan Rickman

Chris Rock

The inside scoop: Emma Thompson was going to play God, but she had to back out. *Dogma* is about a woman who is picked by two renegade angels (guess who?) to save humanity. The great-grandniece of Jesus Christ wreaks havoc by preventing the two angels from reentering Heaven and thus unraveling the fabric of the universe. Got that?

They will also act together in Miramax's *Like a Rock*. "I'm the romantic lead and Matt is supporting—like I was in *Good Will Hunting*," Ben says.

How do they decide—with all those offers flooding in—which movies to make and which ones to pass on? "I say yes when I read the script and say, 'God I wish I'd written that,'" Ben explains. Is he bummed by his busy schedule? "I won't complain. I've known many a day in the past where I had nothing to do but go out and look in the mailbox."

The Scoop on Their Next Screenplay

Halfway House, for Castle Rock, is based on stories pals told the pair about a home for the mentally challenged. Matt plans to play one of the residents. Also set to star is Ben's bro, Casey. "It's an ensemble piece" is all Matt would reveal to *Variety*.

Pop Quiz: *By the Numbers*

So you've read every article you can find on these guys. You've seen each of their movies ten times. You consider yourself their number-one fan. But how fast are you with these figures? There's just one more test before you graduate and become bona fide Matt and Ben experts.

1. How many apartments do Matt and Ben claim to have shared over the years?

   (a) 22
   (b) 6
   (c) 10

2. How many years did it take to write *Good Will Hunting*?
   (a) 10
   (b) 5
   (c) 3

3. How old is Will?
   (a) 18
   (b) 20
   (c) 22

4. What are Matt and Ben's shoe sizes?
- (a) 11 and 13
- (b) 10 and 13
- (c) 10 and 11

5. According to Ben, how much did his *Armageddon* astronaut suit weigh?
- (a) 100 pounds
- (b) a ton
- (c) 200 pounds

Answers: 1. c; 2. b; 3. b; 4. a; 5. c

It's a Wrap

With all their new-found clout (not to mention coolness times two), the sky's the limit for Matt and Ben. Both of their schedules are chock-full for the year ahead, and Hollywood's dynamic duo shows no signs of slowing down on or off screen.

One clue to their future? Maybe Matt said it best:

"We saw our dream come true and that's an amazing feeling. But we're not about to sit back and relax and say, 'Hey. We've done it all. We can retire now.' No way, man. The way we see things, we got a lot of road ahead of us."

Look For These Other Great Titles from HarperActive!

WILL SMITH:

From Fresh Prince to King of Cool
by K. S. Rodriguez

He reigns supreme in television, music, and in the movies, too! Peep out the pages of this book to find out just how Will Smith does it all. His story is the bomb, baby!

THE BACKSTREET BOYS

by K. S. Rodriguez
They're famous, they're hot, and now they're totally yours! Pick up this bio and let the story of the Backstreet Boys drive you wild!